PATH TO PURPOSE

Terri & Layla,

  May God continue to bless you both with all blessings & favor. You're indeed a blessing to the Kingdom. I look forward to seeing what God has for you both next.

          Blessings,
          C. Kelly Brinson

PATH TO PURPOSE

52 WORDS & LIFE APPLICATIONS FOR SELF EMPOWERMENT

CHARLESETTA KELLY BRINSON

Printed in the United States of America
Keen Vision Publishing, LLC
www.publishwithKVP.com
ISBN: 978-1-955316-01-9

***To the younger version of myself,** thank you for all the positive self-talk and belief from the very beginning that whatever we set our mind to accomplish was possible if we never stopped believing in us.*

***In loving memory of my oldest brother, Edward "Bo" Kelley Jr.,** who constantly reinforced my younger version self-talk, with these words of encouragement, "Sis you are strong, you can and will accomplish whatever you choose to do." Big Brother, we are doing it!*

***To my dad, Edward L. Kelley Sr., and my parents Jean and Odis C. Tyree,** thank you for the numerous sacrifices, it is because of those sacrifices I am able to walk in the purpose God has ordained for my life.*

TABLE OF CONTENTS

TABLE OF CONTENTS

PREFACE

Accolades to our Mom and Nana on writing her first book. Growing up we realized her passion for books and reading. We are not surprised she would add to her collections of books with her very own 52 Words & Short Stories.

Growing up, you could always locate a book in our home, and it did not change when the second generation of "Little People" came along. We enjoyed the advanced reading of her book, capturing the essence of the person we call Mom and Nana. We look forward to sharing this book of words and short stories with the second generation of "Little People," giving them a more intimate look into the heart of our Mom and their Nana.

Readers, enjoy your journey through *Path to Purpose.* You will certainly gain valuable insight of what pulls on the heart strings of the woman we call Mom and Nana.

La'toya, Sharee, Nia, Jaida, Leah, Julius, and Ava

ASK

[ask]

Say something to obtain an answer or some information.

There is an old adage: "Don't assume; you make an..." well, we all know the rest. So why do we insist on making assumptions when asking is always an option? Making assumptions instead of asking can lead to misunderstandings. I don't want to mislead you by saying if you ask questions you will initially receive the answers. It could possibly take a series of questions before you arrive at the answers you desire. Maybe we assume rather than ask because asking may require probing questions and transparency. I believe when people feel comfortable with the person inquiring, they are more inclined to respond.

There was once a group of individuals who, I suppose, enjoyed living vicariously through my life events. I recall receiving a phone call two states away from where I was living at that time. On the other end of the phone was my second career mentor. He said, "I just received a call from three states away, asking me something of a personal nature about you." He told the individual they had dialed the wrong number and should call me instead. Any person who knows me well knows that I am transparent on a need-to-know basis. So when the individual finally asked me in person, I said, "Let me ask you a question first."

I asked if providing an answer would help in some manner; I am all about supporting a need. They replied, "No, I just wanted to know." I smiled and politely continued to eat my dinner, seated at the table with the inquiring minded individual. I think after thirty minutes passed, they must have thought I had forgotten; they asked again. This time, I replied, informing them that their desire to know didn't qualify as a need-to-know. I smiled and continued to eat my dinner.

If it's not value-added or for clarification, I don't ask personal questions. Why, you may ask? I have more than enough information occupying my mind already. Why seek more if it's not value-added? Yes, please ask versus assume, but don't waste your ask.

"Quality questions create a quality life. Successful people ask better questions, and as a result, they get better answers."

Anthony Dobbins

BACKDROP

['bak, dräp]

A painted cloth hung at the back of a theater stage as part of the scenery.

W hat is the backdrop of your life story? What has the backdrop of your life set you up for? My belief is that our life story backdrop was set up long before we appeared on the stage of life. I fully embraced the scripture Jeremiah 29:11 "For I know the plans I have for you, declares the Lord, plans to prosper you and not to harm you, plans to give you hope and a future." I believe that God painted the backdrop for my life story. The scenes have changed numerous times, all to support my life story that God has already written. For those of you whose belief system supports that you hung your own backdrop, the question remains the same. What has the backdrop of your life set you up for? Think back on the last movie or maybe live stage play you attended. You saw the characters out front as the movie or play unfolded before you. What you did not see was the preparation and the hanging of the backdrop for the plays, or perhaps digitally displayed for most movies in the 21st Century technology world.

My life story backdrop was painted with the wisdom of

my parents, community, and a village of believers sharing their life stories. Every scene and chapter was not always to their liking, but their trust and faith remained steadfast and unmovable in a faithful God. When a particular scene in my life is not to my liking, I look back at my life story's backdrop. I see it vividly painted with the sweat, tears, hope, and faith of my parents, community, and village of believers. God used them to help shape my life story, according to what Jeremiah penned in Jeremiah 29:11 (NIV). I trust God is working each scene and chapter together for my good according to His purpose, ensuring I arrive at my expected end that He has already written into my life story. No auditions necessary, no body double or substitutes accepted; His original version only. The backdrop has been hung; the curtains have opened. I have taken center stage, and it is show time.

"Once you start recognizing the truth of your story, finish the story. It happened but you're still here, you're still capable, powerful, you're not your circumstance. It happened and you made it through. You're still fully equipped with every single tool you need to fulfill your purpose."

Steve Maraboli

BATON

[ba'tän]

A short stick or tube passed from runner to runner in a relay race.

The phrase "passing the baton" can symbolize many things. The analogy in my writing today is passing the baton between generations. How can each generation determine if their individual and collective actions will contribute to a smooth handoff to the next generation? In a relay race, the handoff is most important; the race will be won or lost based upon the handoff. Similarly, I believe the success and survival of future generations depend on the handoff between them. Research reveals this handoff tip: "Use a visual handoff for the 4x400 and 4x800 relay races; run on the inside part of the lane. Hold the lower half of the baton in your right hand at face height; this allows the outgoing runner to grab the upper half of the baton in his left hand. Let go only when the outgoing runner has a firm grip on the baton."

There are key takeaways from the tip that are worth paying forward. The timing was different, just as each generation's pace or timing is different. I do not believe each generation's pace is as important as simply continuing to move forward.

The precise way the baton is held in the hand of the runner during his or her laps around the track and how it is held during the handoff offers a valuable lesson to us. Just like there is a particular way to hold the baton in both instances, there is also a specific way in which we must take hold of our part when passing the baton from one generation to another.

Each runner is assigned a number based on their running ability. For example, the "Lead Leg" runs the longest, and the "Anchor" runs the shortest. The number assignment is made within the team, and I believe there are similar assignments made within each generation. How are those assignments made within generations? I am going to leave this question on the table for now. My hope is that this question will spark a conversation within each generation and between each generation. Finally, there is a particular place or space in which the baton handoff occurs; the time in the exchange zone area is twenty or thirty meters long. Likewise, there is a particular place or space to pass the baton between each generation, and I believe the time for them both is now. The generation before me (my parents' generation) should be passed the "anchor baton," the shortest; they have run their share of the "lead leg baton," the longest. It is time for my generation to take that baton and allow them to finish the race of life at a slower and enjoyable pace.

"A hundred times every day I remind myself that my inner and outer life depends on the labors of other men, living and dead, and that I must exert myself in order to give in the measure as I have received and am still receiving."

Albert Einstein

BEEP

[bēp]

A short, usually high-pitched sound (as from a horn or an electronic device) serves as a signal or warning.

Four beeps and a pause indicate an emergency, meaning that carbon monoxide has been detected in the area. You should move to fresh air and call 911. One beep every minute indicates a low battery; five beeps every minute indicate the battery's end of life and its time to be replaced. In life, many beeps are seeking our attention. We have the nerve to assist with the beeps in our life by selecting beep tones to recognize who is calling. Sometimes the beeps in life can become distracting to the point we need to silence them. I recall a time when one of my fire detector's batteries needed to be replaced. It started with a faint beep; initially, I could not figure which room it was coming from. I went from room to room, trying to locate the occasional beep; it wasn't until I silenced the other beeps that I could locate it. Sometimes we have to silence some beeps in life that are vying for our attention in order to hear the ones that require our attention the most. Beep!

"Everything beeps now."

George Carlin

BLIND SPOT

['blīn(d)',spät]

An area where a person's view is obstructed.

The television series Blind Spot is about a beautiful young lady who does not know her identity. Her naked body is found in Times Square, with her tattooed body being the only clue for the FBI to discover her true identity. Until her identity was revealed, she was known only as Jane Doe. Jane Doe's blind spot, her obstructed view, can be associated with her loss of identity. Would you agree that we all have at least one blind spot, if not more?

Real talk - transparent moment, one of my blind spots developed early in life. Growing up, my mom taught me and my brother to always seek out the good in people. Her teachings stemmed from her belief in the Bible's instruction for Christians to love others as Christ had loved us. I trusted them to be good, sound teachings. The teachings appeared logical until I came across children and, later, adults who were taught differently. I followed my mom's teaching, as most children would have, throughout my childhood into adulthood. Around forty years later, a credible stranger made a statement in a classroom, and my blind spot was revealed. What was that blind spot? The credible stranger said, "It's perfectly okay to always seek out the good, but do not ignore the bad." In my blind spot, the bad was ignored; by not factoring it into so many decisions, most of the decisions were not in my best interest. The stranger's statement was an eye-opening moment that prompted me to look back at past decisions. I realized if I had factored the bad into the decision equation, in most of those cases, my summation would have been more advantageous.

Going forward, I began removing blind spots. I did not stop seeking out the good; instead, I stopped ignoring the bad. My decisions took on different directions, and my life was filled with more tranquil moments and sustainable decisions. This new place, absent of blind spots, produced clear and sound decisions free of obstructions. Mom's teaching was foundational; I just needed to build upon it. Find and remove your blind spots, and you will see your way in life more clearly.

"The people who would like to manipulate and use you won't tell you your blind spots. They may plan to continue using them to their advantage."

Assegid Habtewold

CAPACITY

[ka'pasadē]

The maximum amount that something can contain.

The importance of knowing the level of your mind capacity is crucial at all times. Your mental health matters. Medical reports today indicate, "The health of the mind is just as important as the health of the body." I carefully chose the word capacity. I wanted to give it the proper, weighted attention in our current COVID-19 pandemic, where so many are reviewing their capacity level. Still, so many continue to ask if mental health really matters and if it should be brought to the forefront of our attention when it comes to holistic health. The World Health Organization (WHO) defines health as "a state of complete physical, mental, and social well-being and not merely the absence of disease or infirmity."

How do we know when or if we are reaching our personal capacity level? A recognition point for me is when I find myself becoming irritated easily. To diffuse the feeling, I personally hit the pause button internally, take some long deep breaths, observe my thoughts, set boundaries, and ask myself if what I'm presently doing is really necessary. If so, I proceed with a clearer mindset after the brief mind pausing exercise. If not, I quickly dismiss the activity and move on to something that eases the mind. I wholeheartedly agree that the health of the mind is just as important as the health of the body.

We must continue to set boundaries and practice proper self-care to protect the mind's healthiness. We need to pave a path to a joyful life that embodies good coping skills, increases our ability to make sound life decisions, and maintains our inner strength.

"More than anything you guard, protect your mind, for life flows from it."

Proverbs 4:23 (CEB)

COMMUNITY

[ka'myoonadē]

A group of people living together in one place, especially one practicing common ownership.

Communities are made up of people who share a sense of place in a given geographical area or virtual space through communication platforms. I was fortunate to grow up in a small, southern Alabama community of unified individuals with common interests living in that area. What were some of the common interests? I am glad you asked. It still fascinates me to share glimpses of a "made for television" childhood, as those who I've shared with call it.

My mom was often called the June Cleaver of the neighborhood. June was the well-put-together mom from the classic television sitcom that aired from 1957-1963. The black and white television sitcom has attained an iconic status in the United States, exemplifying the mid-twentieth century's idealized suburban family. June was the mother of two sons, the older Wally and the younger, inquisitive, and curious Beaver. This stay-at-home mom was rarely ever seen unraveled, despite everything Beaver found himself in daily.

I don't know why Mom was called the June Cleaver of our small southern community. Mom wasn't a stay-at-home mom. She actually worked a full-time job and, on occasion, a part-time job alongside my dad's full-time regular occupation and part-time home business. Mom was also the mother of an older son and a daughter. So why the comparison? Mom, from my perspective, is the epitome of the definition of community. She portrayed the common ownership part as a well-put-together mom, despite her time away from home. She owned her responsibility of motherhood, not only to my brother and me but to any child in the community who needed to be nurtured.

One example of my fondest childhood memories is waking up to the smell of homemade pancakes and bacon that Mom cooked and left warming in the oven before departing for work. She worked on the Army base, which required her attendance at 4:30 a.m. each morning. Mom didn't stop there; she would arrive home approximately one hour before the school bus dropped us off daily.

The kitchen window that faced the highway would be slightly opened, and the aroma of something delicious always met us as we walked up the driveway to the front door. Mom, much like the classic sitcom mom June, added meaning to many generations who had the good fortune of experiencing motherhood's nurturing skills. She so proudly owned and shared.

Mom was and always has been what dictionaries describe as a community: A person among a group of people living together in one place, taking ownership of their skills, and sharing them for others' greater good. I am a proud product of the community, and I believe it's time to bring back the community. It still takes a village or community coming together, owning their skillset, and sharing them for the greater good of all. Are you willing to do your part in bringing back the community?

"The greatness of a community is most accurately measured by the compassionate actions of its members."

Coretta Scott King

COMPARISON

[kam'perasan]

The act of comparing two or more people or things.

How often have you heard that comparison is a thief? According to President Theodore Roosevelt, "Comparison is a thief of joy." When we compare ourselves with others, we allow ourselves to be robbed of authenticity. When I look back over my life, both professionally and personally, I see so many times where I came face to face with comparative measures or challenges against my integrity. The numerous teachings of wisdom in my upbringing solidified my foundation of self-worth. I did not accept offers of compromise that minimize my authenticity. I agree that comparison is a thief of our joy, but it is even a bigger thief than that. If we allow comparison to daily chip away who we are or diminish our integrity, we may wake up and not recognize the person in the mirror. I believe that is too high a cost to pay for comparison.

"Comparison is an act of violence against the self."

Iyanla Vanzant

COMPREHENSION

[,kämpre'hen (t)SH(e)n]

The capacity to fully understand.

To comprehend something is to have the correct explanation of it at present. If you had an accurate understanding of the stock market, could you invest correctly? If you had the correct understanding of which career would support your passion and cause you to climb the success ladder, you would choose it, right? If you had the correct knowledge of encouraging that child who is discouraged, you would encourage them, wouldn't you? The dictionary also stated that when we comprehend, we can fully understand a thing. So I say to you today, you are already enough. You have the capacity and the understanding of who you are and the importance of your existence on the earth right now. It is essential today as you are reading this. You must understand who you are because someone, a family, a community, and ultimately a world is waiting for the full version of who you are and what you bring to the table.

I recall someone asking me once if I comprehended a statement I was making. I immediately responded, "Yes." They asked me the same question again, as though they did not hear my response. So I paused before responding again, "Yes." They said, "I disagree because if you comprehended it, your statement would be followed by an activity." Would you agree that when we comprehend, fully understand a thing, we move toward what we learn? I will leave that question on the table for you to answer at your leisure. At the present moment, I ask that after you have the correct understanding of who you are and what you have to contribute, you don't delay long. There are people waiting for the full capacity and correct version of you to show up. It's time!

"Observing and understanding are two different things."

Mary E. Pearson

CRISIS

['krīsis]

A time when a difficult or important decision must be made.

I'm handling this topic, crisis, with enormous sensitivity in light of our COVID-19 crisis. A famous quote by Winston Churchill reminded me that valuable lessons can be found in a crisis. His saying, "Don't waste a good crisis," was first mentioned by Sir Winston in the mid-1940s, approaching the end of WWII. When I first heard the quote recently, I was slightly puzzled, asking myself "What good is there in a crisis?" I took a closer look at how several individuals in my circle of family and friends were actually extracting the good out of our current crisis that's been termed as a pandemic. I read one particular story that intrigued and inspired me to mention this. It took a particular woman losing her job not only once but twice before she realized the occupation she was looking for was inside of her all along. She launched her own company in the midst of the pandemic and as a result of the pandemic. This woman followed Winston Churchill's quote, and she didn't waste a "good crisis."

Today, I appeal to myself and you as well when I say, "Don't waste a good crisis." Maybe what we have been looking for was never outside of ourselves but was lodged inside of us all the time. Unfortunately, it took a crisis like COVID-19 to reveal what we may have never known if it hadn't invaded our lives in 2020. For those who lost the lives of family members during this crisis, I honor you and your family by not wasting a crisis, extracting the good, supporting those I encounter along the way, and encouraging them to endure in the midst of the crisis.

"Through each crisis in my life, with acceptance and hope, in a single defining moment, I finally gained the courage to do things differently."

Sharon E. Rainey

CROWN

[kroun]

A monarch wore a circular ornamental headdress as a symbol of authority, usually made of or decorated with precious metals and jewels.

The Greek word translated as crown is Stephanos (the source for the name Stephen, the martyr) and means "a badge of royalty, a prize in the public games or a symbol of honor generally." Used during the ancient Greek games, it referred to a wreath or garland of leaves placed on a victor's head as a reward for winning an athletic contest. In today's world, it appears we are void of the comfort level of unity most Americans desire to see. What prompted me to write about the word crown was a phrase I saw stating, "Fix your sister's crown without telling anyone it was crooked." Is it possible for someone to offer support to another person in need without exposing their good deed to everyone else? In other words, can you fix their crown of confidence, lack of self-esteem, ability to use their voice, etc., without bringing the attention to the underdeveloped areas? I believe it's possible, and we should do so always.

People who are a symbol of authority especially take advantage of every opportunity to coach or mentor others in the areas of weakness that may leave their crowns crooked.

The next time you see someone whose life may be a little off balance, see if you can assist them in straightening their crown without bringing it to the attention of anyone else. One day, you may find your crown crooked, and your help will come full circle like the shape of the crown. Someone will help straighten your crown, telling no one.

"Our crown has already been bought and paid for. All we have to do is wear it."

James Baldwin

DECADE

['dekād]

A period of ten years.

Two decades ago, the animated movie Finding Nemo by Walt Disney hit the entertainment world. One decade ago, the recession ended; now, here we are at the beginning of a new decade that began in 2020, in the midst of a pandemic. I heard many say, "I wish we could bypass 2020." I provide a glimpse back two decades to show that in every decade, there is an enjoyable moment like the movie Finding Nemo (2003). However, we were also in a recession, thankfully coming out of it upon entering the next decade (2010). Nearing the end of 2020, we were still in a pandemic.

Decades teach us that there will be both enjoyable and challenging times. If we focus entirely on the challenging times, we may fail to recognize the enjoyable times in our midst. Yes, 2020 was one that caused me to pause on numerous occasions. It will be difficult for analysts to select the top story for 2020; there are so many qualifying stories for that year. Yes, I mourn over 200,000 lives lost to the pandemic and the numerous lives of color lost and undoubtedly disappointed in our country's division. Yet I remain hopeful and thankful for my life and humanity as a whole.

I hope that those remaining, by no goodness of our own, will strengthen that which remains and contribute to making societal and our medical situations better. It is a way we can honor those who did not get a chance. Some believe, depending on the color code entering 1600 Pennsylvania Avenue, our country's societal and medical issues will be resolved. I agree that outstanding leadership is a necessity, and a huge part of ensuring equality and quality of life are afforded to every American. However, we as citizens of this great country are not exempt; we play a part in the change we want to see. No longer uttering the words of change, we must add action to those words to see real change. Decades will happen. Let us not allow them just to happen; let us make them count.

Once you have mastered time, you will understand how true it is that most people overestimate what they can accomplish in a year - and underestimate what they can achieve in a decade!"

Tony Robbins

DIGNITY

['dignadē]

The state or quality of being worthy of honor or respect.

The new buzz words dignity and respect can be heard in almost every news interview, conference room, classroom, boardroom, etc. We are experiencing difficult times that appeared to target people of color and people's societal posture. What is behind the buzz words we hear so frequently today? Dignity and respect are two words that I see and hear used together often. Both words are honorable and noble qualities. I was taught to treat everyone with dignity and respect no matter their skin color or societal standing. A person's worth is not defined by what they do or do not have materially but by the contents of their hearts.

Most organizations include dignity and respect in their equal opportunity policies and training sessions that are mandatory for all leaders. However, what I've seen when forced both as a facilitator and a student, is resistance and grumbling about the training and respect can be mandated for a leader and individuals; however, I believe they should come naturally. Forced behavior produces pretense behavior displayed publicly; however, behind the scenes, the heart is still full of biases toward others. How do we ensure dignity and respect is more than just a check the block or mandated training? We need the words to become a reality that spills over into the hearts of all humanity and into our society. We need to bring authentic and lasting change in our world.

I have seen perspective shifts through revealed bias behaviors during role reverse workshops or training sessions where an individual had to walk in others' shoes. Until you feel the other person's pain and suffering, I believe it will be a check the block, lacking authenticity or changed hearts. One of my favorite R&B singers, Anthony Hamilton, captured it in the song "Walk in My Shoes." The lyric: "If you ever walked a mile in my shoes, you would see what I've been going through... try to walk a mile in my shoes," captures my heartfelt belief. During the sensing sessions, I saw a few tears fall, faces of anger soften, and a smile peek through every now and then. I am not suggesting that years of bias behavior and deep-rooted hatred was changed in a few days. However, I am hopeful that if we show others their words are not harmless but actually impactful and hurtful, it will cause them to stop their behavior for a few hours. I am hopeful that if they consider the ways of others, they may have a change of heart, and I will take that as a small win. I honestly believe every person's desire is to be treated with dignity and respect. Never look down on anyone unless that look is the first step at helping them up.

> **"All labor that uplifts humanity has dignity and importance and should be undertaken with painstaking excellence."**
>
> *Martin Luther King, Jr.*

DOT

[dät]

It is used to refer to an object that appears tiny because it is far away.

Life has been referred to as the children's game known as connecting the dots, fun for children and adults alike. The object of the game is to connect the dots to reveal the big picture. The game was created by someone who knew what the big picture would reveal, how many dots are necessary per page, and strategically placed them on each page. So how are the dots in our life connected to reveal the big picture? Allow me to refer to our lives as the dots, the paper as the world we are placed upon, and God as the author. He strategically placed the dots around the globe, which connects them to the appropriate time, revealing the big picture of life already present in His mind. He is the holder of the pen with the knowledge of when and what dots need to be connected. What is our role as the dot? Trust the one who holds the pen with big picture faith; He is, after all, the author and finisher of our faith.

"You have to trust that the dots will somehow connect in your future."

Thomas L. Friedman

EMPTY WORD

['em(p)tē werd]

A word that has a grammatical function and has no meaning in itself.

You, like myself, have probably sat through numerous speeches, briefings, and workshops filled with empty words. What makes words empty? If you take away its grammatical function, it has nothing to stand upon. Empty words can be something said void of emotions. I will not ask the question, "Are you guilty of speaking empty words." Instead, I will say that we have all been guilty of speaking empty words. When was the last time you said, "Have a good day," and did not mean it? Perhaps it was to a person identified to be rude or bias to your race. Honestly, did you mean that, or was it just the polite or political thing to say? Should we have remained silent with a slight smile of acknowledgment in passing, rather than spewing out empty words, as innocent as they may have been? Well, it depends on who your audience is. Some audiences almost demand a polite or political response, even if they're empty words.

What's amazing to me is our society appears to have grown accustomed to accepting empty words rather than no response at all. I noticed that people quickly become judgmental, saying, "Oh, how rude," after observing someone saying good morning and it was met with no response. What if I told you that you may not be privileged to know the back story for the lack of response? Like me, you may be often guilty of saying, "What harm is it to say good morning or thank you?" Well, the harm may very well be that we are encouraging more empty words into the atmosphere.

I had a co-worker once known throughout the building to never respond to anyone. On occasion, caught by surprise, I would say good morning with true sincerity; however, to be met with unpleasant facial expressions challenged me. So I started making eye contact with a smile. The smile was a reminder for me to continue having a great morning. Perhaps her words, if spoken, would've been empty with no added value. Who knows? I did speak these words silently in prayer, "God, be the voice she will respond to." My goal is to always ensure my professional and personal life audio and video match. Whatever you hear me saying, I want to be sure you always see me doing. I never want to appear full and be found empty; my contents matter.

"Let no man deceive you with empty words."

Ephesians 5:6 (RSV)

FIT

[fit]

(Of a thing) of a suitable quality, standard, or type to meet the
required purpose.

Webster defines fit as changing (something) to make it suitable for a new use or situation. I agree changing a piece of clothing or furnishing for a proper fit or usage is ideal. However, I suggest we research first, beginning inwardly before trying to fit in places that are not in our best interest. A new phrase I have learned to appreciate more as I mature is, "We are the owners of our lives." We cannot expect others to take ownership. Yes, ask for guidance or assistance, and I highly recommend it for effectiveness. Trust yourself, yes, but verify authenticity with a trustworthy confidant. Many people have our best interest in mind; however, no person other than yourself can define your fit in life because no one spends more time with you than you do. I am not suggesting spending time alone guarantees knowledge, but time well spent includes honest, transparent self-talk. Be willing to have the tough conversations, perhaps those we have never had with anyone.

Come to terms with knowledge gained, and be okay with what is discovered, even those unwise choices or missed opportunities that may have been plaguing you for years.

I hope we learned some valuable lessons, mainly when we were not meant to fit in every place available or offered. Why do we so desperately try to fit in when we were made to stand out? Over the years of searching my life stories, I found earlier chapters where I considered fitting in. In my late twenties, I had an epiphany and realized my false sense of considering the need to fit in had very little to do with others. It had everything to do with me briefly downsizing who I was for others to feel comfortable with themselves. During that brief period, I had made others' needs and feelings a high priority and my own an occasional option. You are the owner of your life; take ownership seriously. Look within your heart, see the real you, and discover what you want. Write your vision statement for others to follow. There is nothing wrong with having a hierarchy to assist and appointing someone as Chief Executive Officer (CEO), whose primary role is to help you oversee day-to-day activities in line with your vision as the owner. Fitting in is not designed for individuals who're destined to stand out. That is us.

> **"To be yourself in a world that is constantly trying to make you something else is the greatest accomplishment."**
>
> *Ralph Waldo Emerson*

FLIRT

[flert]

Experiment with or show a superficial interest in (an idea, activity, or movement) without committing oneself to it seriously.

T he first thought that comes to mind when you hear the word flirt or flirting is most likely to amuse oneself, play with, or entertain the idea of something or someone. Let me ask you something; and rest assure, I have asked myself this same question. When will you stop flirting with life and at least move on to dating and ultimately committing to it? For years, I entertained the idea of living my authentic life without actually living it. Why would someone do such a thing? Well, my why was summed up in expectations of others and unrealistic expectations of myself? Maybe unrealistic expectation is too strong a word, so I'll say expectations or desires that were misplaced and never intended for my ownership. Why do we, as individuals, feel inclined to fulfill expectations that are not ours to own? Honestly, I cannot give a definitive answer for myself. I don't think it is because we care too much for others, but it's because we don't care enough for ourselves.

A life event brought me closer to a more definitive answer when a relative said, "I will just die; I will not live," if

I didn't make the decision they were expecting. Not once did they ask me how or why I had to make the decision or what would happen to me if I didn't make it. In their statement, I was removed from the decision, although the decision was very much about me. I found the voice I had been flirting with for years. That day, I stopped hitting my internal alarm's snooze button, and I awakened to my authentic self. I voiced something audibly for the first time after so many conversations about it in my mind. I responded, "If I don't make this decision, it could cost my life - a life of authenticity."I urge anyone flirting with life to stop. At the least, start dating life on a regular and hopefully, one day, you will commit to the authentic life of your dreams.

"Traveling is like flirting with life. Be watchful, you may fall in love with life."

Author Unknown

FOCUS

['fōkus]

The center of interest or activity.

My core beliefs are derived from my spiritual upbringing in a small family church and life application teachings at home. I grew up in the beauty of country life, surrounded by walnut trees, vegetable gardens, fruit orchards, horses, and dairy cattle running in the fields nearby. It was free of what I would later learn: distracting noises. The sounds that awakened me in the morning were birds chirping outside my window or cattle mooing in a nearby field. I fell asleep to almost complete quietness of the night. Occasionally, there would be the sound of what my elders termed the old hoot owl, and they believed the owl's hoot was some type of message for the listening ears. Even his strange sound, on occasions, did not prevent me from falling asleep.

My childhood's simplistic beauty was difficult to let go of. So when my childhood gradually came to an end and I hesitantly entered adulthood, I encountered sounds I termed as distracting noises in most instances. I termed it distracting noises because, unlike my childhood, most of the sounds were no longer comforting but disturbing. They challenged my ability to focus. What can a person do to regain focus with so many things and people vying for our attention? Something that works for me is traveling back to my childhood environment, sitting on the porch of the elders basking in the soothing sounds of my childhood that remains. Unfortunately, I cannot always retreat to this environment physically when overwhelming feelings begin to arise. At times, I'm unable to retreat. I tap into the imaginative little girl and visionary woman. I briefly close my eyes and retreat there in my mind.

It is important to operate from a place of focus. Why? Research reveals that being focused promotes clear goals and objectives, and you are most likely dedicated to achieving those goals and objectives in focus. The area of focus I wrestle with the most is focus in the present moment. Why? My imaginative and visionary traits are constantly wooing me to take a journey past the "focus on the present moment" to future places. If the wooing becomes overwhelming, I take self-care moments, days, or just one day, shutting down everything to allow my mind to rest along with my body. The reason I say along with my body is because my body rests every night; however, my mind does not necessarily shut down along with my body each night. I learned this when I would awaken tired after plenty of sleep. I went to a medical professional and was told that I'm missing a mineral that prevents an area of the brain from shutting down, and therefore, I wake up tired. She prescribed a liquid vitamin, and within a few days, I was mentally resting along with my body. I leave this life lesson with you: put yourself at the top of your accomplish list and take a self-care day or days to establish or regain your focus. Improve your focus; increase productivity.

"Your life is controlled by what you focus on."
Tony Robbins

FORECAST

['fôr,kast]

A prediction or estimate of future events, especially coming
weather or a financial trend.

Forecasting is a process in which making predictions
for the future is based on a past or present information
trend. It is interesting how meteorologists can predict
a ten-day forecast, and in most instances, they are reasonably
accurate. However, they can only predict based on past and
present data. Even with the best data, sometimes the weather
chooses a different path from past or present trends. It
doesn't matter how accurate the meteorologist is. It is still a
prediction based on the validity of the past and present data
available.

Standardized testing is a way for students to be evaluated
on a state and national level. I have always been hesitant
to accept the test as one for all and true for all. When my
oldest child was in elementary school, immediately after
returning from overseas, she took a standardized test. She
was and always had been a straight-A student, speaking
two languages at that particular time. However, her teacher
wanted to label and assign her classwork level accordingly,
based on the scoring of one standardized test that stated she

was below the state and national percentile. No worries; it did not happen.

My daughter graduated with honors from high school in the top ten percent of her graduating class. She went on to college with a full academic scholarship, graduating four years later with a Chemistry degree. The standardized test forecasted weak areas that were actually always her strongest areas: math, science, and reading comprehension. The one thing the standardized test did not factor in was her nervousness that arose when taking a timed test. It's something she managed, but I'm not sure if she ever really overcame the nervousness.

Just like the person who forecasts the weather, even though they have strong past and present trends, sometimes the weather goes against what has been forecasted. The next time someone attempts to forecast or predict what you can or cannot do based on a set of trends, remind them that forecasting is only a prediction and not a concrete fact. Then go against those forecasts and be great anyway.

Life is 10% of what happens to us and 90% how we react to it."

Dennis P. Kimbro

FOSTER

['fäster]

Encourage or promote the development of (something, typically something regarded as useful).

H ave you fostered an environment for _____? I will allow you to fill in the blank for yourself. My word in the blank is growth. Have I fostered an environment that's conducive for others to grow into the best version of themselves? Well, through coaching and mentoring, I do. A question was posed to me years ago: "What does your ideal career look like?" Before I answered, the Human Resource Director went on to say, "I'm not asking you what title or pay scale." She asked me to picture myself sitting in the office; what did I see and feel while sitting there? What was I contributing to the organization or perhaps my own business? She gave me some additional time by saying, "I'm not asking you to answer the question now or even to me; I want you to answer for yourself, then pursue the path the answer provides you."

I have never been an individual who is driven by money. Let me explain my position before your emotions take over. I applied for my first position at the age of sixteen. I wanted to do something that would allow my limited skill set, at that time, to contribute to the organization – something they could build upon, in turn. In my sixteen years, I had already learned I interacted well with people, and I felt rewarded when I helped people. It also helped me become a better version of myself.

In elementary and middle school, I was the little girl on the playground playing the mediator rather than on the monkey bars and merry-go-round. I wanted my classmates to play nicely so everyone could have fun.

The little girl in me still plays the mediator and advocate for those who shy away from their own voices. She is fostering an environment full of harmony so others can become the best version of themselves.

So to answer the questions asked earlier on, yes, I believe I foster such an environment. My ideal career looks a lot like my current career over the last thirty-five years. My skill set is value-added and positions the organization better than I found it. It is one where I've departed a better version of myself than I arrived. That can be mostly attributed to being driven by a passion for helping people and not driven by a career that could fill my bank account. It can be attributed to being in a space that fostered an environment for me and generations coming behind me or even walking beside me. So I challenge you, if you're not currently doing so already, to foster an environment that's bigger than you. I have found that when I pursued my passion, the money followed me. Fostering matters.

"What you do makes a difference, and you have to decide what kind of difference you want to make."

Jane Goodall

HALFWAY

['haf,wā]

At or to a point equidistant between two others.

Kenny Loggins, a soft rock singer, released the album titled Back to Avalon. On the album, is the #11 hit single in the United States titled "Meet Me Halfway," which plays for three minutes and thirty-nine seconds long. The song is about a man, obviously in love, asking the woman who held his heart to meet him halfway at the borderline. He expressed to her that he couldn't go any further but would wait until he dies, pleading with her to tell him where she wanted to meet. Have you ever been in a discussion and you hear someone make the statement, "Meet me halfway"? This statement can be defined differently based on the situation or discussion. When it is obvious in a discussion that an agreement will not be reached, I say, "Let's agree to disagree and move on from here." It works approximately 98% of the time, and the other 2% remaining is where I find myself engaged with individuals who are unwilling to meet me halfway or anything other than all of their way.

Choosing how we utilize our energy is crucial. We should save our energy for things that matter in life for us, our family, and our friends. If it adds no value or positivity, save your energy. If it is someone or something that has to be addressed, analyze the personality types involved and utilize effective tactics to bring a win-win for yourself and the project. The most significant challenges in my thirty-five plus year career are never the complexities of the project I lead but the gruesome personalities I have to endure. I define myself as a drama-free individual, both professionally and personally. However, professionally, I tolerate the smallest amount of "fluff" to the point necessary to remain politically correct. Integrity is never up for negotiation. I am willing to come to the table halfway; however, I am not willing to sit in the seat of deceit, the seat of degradation, or seats that lack integrity and authenticity. If you are ever asked to meet at the table halfway, make sure you understand what is on the table before taking a seat. It could cost you all of your integrity.

"Believe you can, and you're halfway there."
Theodore Roosevelt

HOMEGROWN

[ˌhōmˈgrōn]

It is grown or produced in one's own garden or country.

I have always been attracted to the term homegrown, especially regarding agriculture, growing of fruits and vegetables. I grew up in an environment where everything came from the ground, and very little of what we consumed came out of a can, box, or fast food restaurant. Did you ever wonder why it's called "fast food"? I have heard the phrase "we live in a microwave generation." If what we seek isn't delivered quickly, in a hurry, we instantly become impatient and move on to something or someone who can provide it quicker. Well, maybe my upbringing taught me the valuable lesson of patience. Entering into planting season, a preparation process of the ground had to take place. It took tilling the soil and adding fertilizer to ensure the ground was prepared for planting to produce a good crop. So today, I ask you, "Are you homegrown? Are the generations following us homegrown?" Did your parents or grandparents, aunts, uncles, and community help prepare your ground with good character traits, discipline, respect, and appreciation for your life and humanity as a whole?

Now back to the patience and preference. Watching the process of the ground being tilled and fertilized challenged me often, but it quickly turned into excitement when I saw the plants starting to peek through the dirt and begin yielding fruits and vegetables. I think watermelon is a fascinating process for me; you get to see such a tiny seed produce a large tasty watermelon. The lesson I want to drive home to parents, grandparents, uncles, aunts, teachers, and communities is to never underestimate the size of the seed you plant into those prepared lives. They're grounded and will produce big things in their season. You have laid the groundwork that will develop or expand in the future. Rest assured, your labor wasn't in vain. Sit back with patience and excitement, watching your work produce big things.

"You will enjoy the fruit of your labor. How joyful and prosperous you will be!"

Psalms 128:2 (NLT)

LIGHT

[līt]

The natural agent that stimulates sight and makes things visible.

The light bulb naturally provides light in a room of darkness. Like the light, human beings have a natural way of shedding light on the path for others. I believe the life experiences on our paths prepare us to be the light that stimulates sight for our paths and the paths of others. We have to be willing to share our light of successes and our light of lessons learned through our failed efforts. Our light serves as directional signs, much like road signs on a highway.

This reminds me of a road trip from Mississippi where the road sign read, "Rough road next five-ten miles." I had never seen that particular sign before, but I thought, "How bad could it be if the road remained open?" The warning sign was applied to both lanes, so I had no choice but to drive through it. The more I drove, the rougher the road became; my hazard tire sign started flashing on my vehicle. Still, no way around it and unable to pull over, all I could do was keep going. I took the first exit in a safe location after the rough areas ended. I paused for a moment and regained my composure, only to get out of the car to watch my tire deflate before my eyes. I was not discouraged but glad to be safe. I got back into the car and called roadside assistance. The first question they asked was, "Are you in a safe place?" I replied yes, and they asked, "Where are you located?" I could not answer that question because I did not get a chance to see the exit number during the abrupt exit off. He asked a follow-up question. "What do you see?" I looked around and noticed a light coming from a familiar restaurant, so I provided that information and help was on the way.

Life is sometimes like that road trip. We encounter some unexpected rough patches, finding ourselves in some unfamiliar places that we cannot go around. With only one choice, we must go through. During those times, before you panic, pause and regain your composure. Look around for a person carrying the light that stimulates your sight, providing visibility to your path that could quickly aide in the arrival at your destined place.

"Give light and people will find their way."

Ella Baker

MENTOR

['men,tôr]

An experienced and trusted adviser.

I became a product of mentoring. The importance of pairing at the onset of the relationship is crucial to a successful mentorship. Early on in my job, I joined a professional organization to develop my skillset and learn how to manage my career effectively. I am a supporter by nature, so when committees formed in areas of interest in the organization, I quickly offered assistance. One day, an individual I termed as a foundational father figure of the organization stopped me between classes and asked me this question: "When are you going to stop hiding in the background and take your seat out front?" I was speechless because I had great respect for him. He went on to say, in my silence, "I have been watching you support others' platform, and now it is time for you to come from the background and find your platform." That was the beginning of my first mentoring relationship.

On any given day, I might receive an email with a thought-provoking quote, usually about the civil rights, equal opportunity, and justice. He was a huge advocate for equal rights for all. On occasion, the email would be followed up with a brief phone call saying, "Young lady, I'm on the road to a particular area to help fight for justice for one of our brothers or sisters in a struggle, what was your takeaway from the quote I sent you?" I'm not sure if you ever heard that you should have a postcard-ready response that you can verbalize in less than sixty seconds. That was about how much time I had to respond. This taught me to be brief but detailed – one of the most significant takeaways from our mentor-mentee relationship.

Mentoring has and continues to be critical in my professional and personal life. I am paying forward valuable knowledge gained throughout my professional career, personal life, and lessons learned from my mentors. It is rewarding when I see them take the knowledge up a notch or two and define success in their way. Here are ten steps I often utilize in my mentor-protégé relationship is as follows:

1. Set clear and concise expectations

2. Establish mutual accountability

3. Celebrate milestones through lunch and learn sessions,

4. Empower; do not solve the challenges

5. Be intentional of the time and energy I invest into the relationship

6. Know my worth as well as my limitations; know when to bring a subject matter expert into the relationship

7. Share opportunities for growth both professionally and personally

8. Learn from each other; give and take

9. Open doors of opportunity

10. Respect differences.

You may be questioning if you should have a mentor or if you are qualified to be a mentor; absolute yes. Mentoring matters, regardless of what end of the spectrum you find yourself. What you take for granted may be invaluable knowledge to someone else.

> **"Life's most persistent and urgent question is,
> 'What are you doing for others?'"**
>
> *Martin Luther King, Jr.*

NEUROPLASTICITY

[n(y) o orō pla stis dē]

The capacity of the brain to develop and change throughout life,
something Western science once thought impossible.

Scientific research once thought neuroplasticity was
impossible. Now, numerous say there is no expiration
date for the brain to stop developing and changing
throughout a lifetime. If research is proven to be accurate,
the old adage we often hear, "It's never too late to change your
mind," could be relevant to what I am about to say. We live in
a time where people live longer and still achieve success at
ages once thought impossible or at least unheard of.

Nola Ochs, Guinness World Record holder of the world's
oldest graduate at age ninety-five with a 3.7 GPA, didn't see her
age as an obstacle but an opportunity. Many say that Nola's
education got sidetracked after marrying her husband, and
the realities of farming took precedent. After her husband
passed, she returned to pursue her education. One might
say she changed her mind; perhaps it was just her brain
recycling and bringing back to the forefront what had always
been there. Whatever caused Nola to pursue something she
once considered and started some forty-eight years prior is
not my real focus. My real focus is that Nola proved it's never

too late to live your dream, and you're never too old to learn something new.

I don't seriously think Nola set out to be listed in the Guinness Book of Records; she probably just wanted to finish something she once started. By the time Nola passed away in 2016 at 105 years old, she had achieved her goal of writing a book about her life. Is there something you started that you have yet to finish? Have you said to yourself, "It's too late," or "I'm too old"? Hopefully, Nola's story ignites something in your brain today. Let it ignite the spirit of a finisher so you can change your mind, realizing it's not too late to finish what you started, even if the start was only in your mind. Get started and get finished!

"I don't dwell on my age. It might limit what I can do. As long as I have my mind and health, age is just a number."

Nola Ochs

NO

[nō]

Not at all, to no extent.

We live in a world where we hear the word no so often that we begin looking at the word negatively. All noes are not harmful, just as all yeses are not favorable. Some individuals have difficulty saying no, especially to family and friends. We have to pause and rethink our yeses when helping others begins to hurt ourselves. My graduation plan for saying no without guilt is softening it with phrases like "No, not this time," "No, maybe next time," or "With regrets, I have to say no at this time." If you have filled your family and friends' room with yeses most of your life, it will require some transitioning because even your reluctant yes was better than a no. Brace yourself and stand firm on your noes; there may be some sad faces, some guilt trips, and emotions you did not know existed before. Speaking from experience, eventually, others will learn to respect your noes. It is probably never as much as you will, but hopefully, it leaves you guilt-free if you've felt guilty.

Have you ever noticed a toddler or young child's emotional response when you tell them no? Where did they learn the behavior? I have seen loud sobbing, screaming, temper tantrums, and holding their breath until noes are replaced with a yes or okay. I wonder if giving a yes in place of a no is best for the child. I have heard it stop the behavior for the short term. However, the bigger question for me is how it will affect the child long term. Does this encourage repeated behavior not only in children but adults alike? I've even watched leaders and individuals who have a poor work ethic appear helpless and offer excuses for certain behavior. After looking closer at a few scenarios from a professional perspective, I realized the root cause of the problem was they had way too many yeses and not enough noes. This affirmed what I stated earlier about the comfortability level of using the word no when necessary. Is it just a phase children and adults will grow out of? Did our short-term content fix the issue or perpetuate a more significant long-term problem? Scrutinize each situation, weigh the pros and cons of what is short terms vs. long term, then let your noes be noes and your yeses be yeses. Your noes now could eliminate years of regrets later. Short term vs. long term – you decide.

"Be the person who creates positive ripple effects."

Camilla Kragius

PAIN POINT

[peyn-point]

At the root, a pain point is something frustrating or a troublesome issue. It's a problem waiting for a solution. I chose the term pain point because I believe our pain point directs us to our purpose. So I tested the theory on one of my pain points, the erosion of childhood innocence. I found my passion for helping preserve the innocence of our children, starting with my children. Once, I attended a child's birthday party with my children. When I scanned the room, I found very few children besides the birthday child and maybe two other kids. No big deal, correct? I did not see any balloons, birthday cake, prize bags, or anything for children in the room where I was seated My concerns grew as more adults started to arrive with alcoholic beverages. The music turned from songs like "SpongeBob Square Pants" to music with explicit language. I scanned the room, and no one seemed bothered; as a matter of fact, some of the children started to sing the lyrics along with the adults. Wow!

Our children's innocence is being hijacked. I have seen

so many children like the children at the birthday party who can repeat explicit lyrics but cannot recite their alphabets and can barely spell their names. How do we change this type of real-life scenario? I still believe it takes a village. I agree the village may need revamping, but I believe it still exists and is still necessary.

A rocking chair is often symbolic to children, innocence, and comfort. Someone said, "Few children will resist the rocking chair or being rocked." Years ago, and perhaps still today, young mothers included a rocking chair in their nursery design. I continue to see the erosion of children's innocence, and my mind reflects the rocking chair. I question if I'm willing to be a symbolic rocking chair to bring comfort and help preserve our children's innocence. My response is a resounding yes. I believe a healthy future depends on protecting the innocence of our children; they deserve an environment that will allow them to transition into adulthood mentally and physically whole. How do we begin? I'm starting here.

**"The sun illuminates only the eye of man,
but shines into the eye and the heart of the child."**

Ralph Waldo Emerson

PICTURE

[pik (t)SH r]

Represent (someone or something) in a photograph or picture.

W e've often heard the idiom "the big picture," which implies an overall or long-range view of a situation where, in most instances, specific details have been omitted in favor of presenting a more limited view. Why would anyone want a limited view when the big picture view is available? I am a big picture individual, attracted to ideas and projects that provide the big picture view. I'm slightly uncomfortable making a decision with only a limited view. The leader in me ponders over who or what will be affected in my decision making, hence why I desire the big picture view. I remember being called into a meeting without an agenda, having no idea of the subject matter. I took my seat at the table with a group of leaders who presented a proposal they wanted me to sign. Numerous thoughts went through my mind after I noticed everyone had read advanced copies.

When I inquired, apologies flew throughout the room, with all eyes on me as I attempted to read and comprehend the copy handed to me. I glanced at the limited view paper; it was very vague. I asked for a bigger picture view and was met with long, silent stares. I provided a response that wasn't in agreement but obviously one they had prepared for. The senior leader offered many accolades ahead of a promising future promotion if I signed off on the decision; I declined. He was shocked and asked my reason for declining. My response hinged on the fact that the decision and offer went against my leadership style of serving others and lent itself toward self-service. The decision would've served me well but excluded the team I served – a picture that didn't represent me in the big picture view. Life doesn't always present us with the picture of our choice; be sure you don't lose yourself in the picture presented.

"If you think you are the entire picture, you will never see the big picture."

John C. Maxwell

PLATFORM

[platfŏrm]

A set of values for which he or she is (or will become) known.

I believe every person has to take a stand for something that matters to them at some point in their life. During those crucial moments, do your set of values instantly stare you in the face? Reflecting on my set of values, I realize that my parents established the strongest ones during my youth. When my daughters were growing up, I chose my words carefully. I hoped doing so would help build a strong set of values for them to stand upon - values that would shape two little girls into independent women who would always remain true to themselves.

One word that was not always easy to say during child-rearing was the word no. This word resulted in many sad faces; some of those sad faces were filled with tears. The tears almost made me consider changing the answer to a yes. Standing there looking into those cute little faces, my set of values came flooding into my mind reminding me of my platform as a mom. My responsibility was to raise my children to be independent adults and teach them to know their worth, understand respect, appreciate humanity, and leave the world a little better off than they found it. Despite the pain associated with staying true to my own set of values, I realized that they would grow up one day. Learning the importance of no later in life would probably be more painful for them. Yes, your set of values will be challenged, but staying true to them will help preserve your authenticity, leaving the world a little better than you found it.

"Well, if you're true to yourself you're going to be true to everyone else."

John Wooden

PREOCCUPIED

[prē- ä-ky - pīd]

Previously applied to another group and unavailable for use in a new sense.

Living in a preoccupied world is not living in real time. It's a fictional future that keeps you from enjoying the present moment, something as simple as relaxing to the point of not thinking about anything. Preoccupation pushes us into a mindset where we are trying to address something before it is time. Why do you think individuals live preoccupied with their tomorrows? If we are not careful, we will allow our concerns to cripple us permanently; we'll become stuck in that fictional future. It is often believed that 90% of future problems in our imaginary or fictional world never happens. A western country song titled "Meant to Be" simplifies this whole preoccupied state of mind for me. A particular portion of the lyrics says, "If it's meant to be, it'll be. Baby, just let it be. So, won't you ride with me, ride with me? See where this thing goes. If it's meant to be, it'll be; Baby, if it's meant to be."

Years ago, I recalled being so preoccupied with a situation that was not mine but indirectly affected me. I allowed it to drag my mind into this fictional world for days until one day,

I asked myself a series of questions: "What is the worst thing that can happen? If that happens, could you handle it?" My response was yes. Suddenly, the preoccupation ceased and life, in that moment, instantly became more enjoyable. So why did I allow it to keep me preoccupied for days before addressing it? I'm not exactly sure, but I think because it involved the quality of life for someone other than myself. If you learn from a loss, you did not lose but learned a life lesson. The next time your thoughts attempt to carry you to that fictional world, worrying about future problems that never happen 90% of the time, stop and tell yourself, "If it's meant to be, let it be."

"I always live in the present. The future, I can't know. The past I no longer have."

Fernando Pessoa

PRESENT

[prez( )nt]

It is occurring right now.

We live in a world where multitasking is fully embraced and often rewarded as a vital skill set for those who possess it. For the past thirty-five years and some, my life has involved a career environment where you're already behind in strategic planning if you're living in the present. Technology is an excellent example of this. By the time the latest and greatest cell phone is released, the developers have already begun working on, if not already completed, the next generation of technology.

A few years ago, I had an epiphany while sitting in my living room, working on a class assignment. I thought I was working on my assignment until I looked down at my essay and noticed I had captured tomorrow's assignment, along with family concerns. Wow! At that very moment, I realized I wasn't fully present or totally working on my assignment. After taking a break and checking off a few things on my list and in my mind, I went back to my writing assignment. My thoughts flowed easier, and the essay was completed free of things not relevant to the assignment. Yes, I'm good at multitasking. I am great at project management to forecast years beyond the present moment, something my current career requires and often demands. My takeaway from the epiphany was, "Young lady, you're not very effective living in the present moment." When you spend eight to ten hours working daily, you think about things a certain way. I'm being generous on the hours because it covers the amount of time we physically spend in the office, but we also mentally bring the office work home.

In October of 2004, to rectify or strengthen my ability to live in the present moment more, I purchased and began reading The Power of Now by Eckhart Tolle. Tolle asked, "What's going on inside me at this moment? That question will point you in the right direction. But don't analyze, just watch. Focus your attention within." I answered Tolle's question with this response, "It's October 10, 2004; professionally, I'm four years into a gratifying career change. However, I agreed with one of my mentors that I had stayed in my last assignment too long. Personally, I felt overjoyed, having just attended two graduations two weeks apart.

My oldest daughter graduated from college with a Chemistry degree and entered into a pre-medicine program, and the youngest graduated from high school and is now settled into college to pursue a degree in Biology. For the last twenty-two years, all of my present moments were focused on two original little people – a term of endearment for my two young ladies. Most of those moments were focused on providing a strong foundation for them to build upon to become successful at whatever they chose to do in life. So from that evening in 2004 to this day, I've made a huge stride in living and enjoying more present moments.

Regretfully, I missed out on numerous enjoyable "aha" present moments. However, I don't count them as lost moments but lessons learned. Moving forward, I'm enjoying more present moments. So you, yes you reading now, I challenge you to silence everything around you. Wherever you are, fully be there both mentally and physically. The present moment is the only guaranteed moment we have; not one moment later is guaranteed. Let us live in the right now, a place that has been waiting on our arrival most of our lives. Enjoy it!

"You are here to enable the divine purpose of the Universe to unfold. That is how important you are!"

Eckhart Tolle

ROOM

[ro om]

Space that can be occupied or where something can be done,
especially viewed in terms of whether there is enough.

When the word *room* is mentioned, what are the first things that come to mind? For myself, I think of location, capacity, contents, and view. I wanted to write my first book on something I am passionate about: words and their definitions. I sat in a room that I call my reading room or accent room. It is vibrant in color and separated, far away from the other ten rooms in my home. The room is a very accurate reflection of a quiet, peaceful space within myself. It is decorated with bright orange, lemon yellow, Scandinavian wood, glass, African art, oil paintings, family and special friends' pictures, family trophies recognizing their many achievements, and highlighted by the antique tea set from Bavaria that my mom gave me. The lemon leather sofa, draped by a soft infinity throw and accented by two tiger orange Bogart chairs, continues to bring me so many enjoyable moments while sitting in the quietness of this room tucked away in the corner of my home.

Taking time to vividly describe the room that reflects so much of who I am was intentional. I hope the glimpse of the room allows you to sense the peace the room provides; the contents have been carefully placed in this room that is still becoming, like myself, the best version. I find peace in the strength and suppleness of the leather, the softness of the infinity throw, the firmness and the snuggling embrace of the tiger orange Bogart chairs. These things surrounded by what matters to me the most: family and close friends and so many items that reflect my travels around the world bring peace and comfort to internal rooms of my life.

It has been said, our outward environment is a reflection of what is happening inwardly. If this is indeed a fact, the room tells my story accurately. Many suggestions have been offered for additions to complete this room. I'm in agreement that the room is still becoming, just as I am; however, I am cautious of what is placed in this room and in my life. The desired goal is always protecting the peace not just filling the space.

"Your sacred space is where you can find yourself over and over again."

Joseph Campbell

SAY WHEN

[sā] [(h)wen]

Utter words to convey information, an opinion, a feeling or intention, or an instruction. At what time?

Have you ever wondered why a waiter or waitress, when pouring your drink, says to you, "Say when," to alert them when to stop pouring? They are looking at the same glass you're looking at, so why would they need to tell you to "say when." The glass capacity is identical from both perspectives; however, what is different is the level you want the glass to be filled. Just as the glass has a capacity level of what it can hold, so do we as individuals.

It would be nice if people would ask us or respect us when we say when. There are not many occasions when someone will ask you to "say when," so I challenge you never to be afraid to utilize your voice to say when. Just because you may have the capacity to hold more doesn't mean you should be filled to capacity every time.

I have dined at certain restaurants where the server never allows my cup to reach below its capacity. Initially, it is okay, but after I have eaten a large amount of my food, my cup's necessity to be filled to capacity lessens. I've had to stay alert when the server came to fill my glass; sometimes I've had to place my hand over my glass. Eventually, I would tell the server, "I'm good, I don't need my glass to be refilled."

It is no different in our individual lives. We have to stay alert when people come to fill our vessels with doubt, stress, negativity, etc. You may have to even go beyond saying when by covering yourself, your mind, and your mental capacity. If you're getting the message later than sooner, it's never too late to begin again, in a positive way, by never being afraid to "say when."

"Do something today your future self will thank you for."

Sean Patrick Flanery

SILENCE

[sīl ns]

The complete absence of sound.

The world-famous Anechoic Chamber, located in Redmond, Washington, is the quietest place on earth. The cost for entrance into the chamber of silence is approximately $125 per person. It is believed our ears and brains are starved for input when placed in silence. The brain and ears will go into overdrive, seeking information to the point you may hear your breathing, your heartbeat, and your blood pumping to your head. Science says noise creates stress while silence relieves stress and tension and is necessary for our overall well-being. If silence is necessary for our well-being, why do we seek ways to replace silence with noise?

In 2011, the World Health Organization (WHO) examined and quantified its health burden in Europe. It concluded that the 340 million residents of Western Europe (about the United States population) were losing a million years of healthy life every year due to noise. WHO also said that the root cause of 3,000 heart disease deaths was due to excessive noise. The word noise comes from the Latin word nausia (disgust or nausea) or the Latin word noxia, meaning hurt, damage, or injury. Silence has so many positive attributes, and yet we live in a society that does not seem to appreciate its benefits.

When was the last time you sought out the good company of complete silence? Unbelievably, the most quiet I have ever experienced was at a 5-star hotel in New York City. I am not sure what type of walls or doors the hotel structure was made of, but when you closed the door, it was as though you shut the world and its noises outside. I closed the room darkening curtains, turned out all the lights, and enjoyed hours of silence to the point when I awakened in the middle of the night. I was often startled at first, having relaxed to the point that I forgot I had flown to New York a few hours or days prior. I looked forward to the end of each workday to shut out the world and its noises outside. I suppose a city nicknamed "The City That Never Sleeps" had to find a way to silence the noisiness for those who wanted to sleep. It may not be easy to locate a New York City-style silence. Whenever possible, seek out ways to incorporate silence in your lifestyle. Your mental and physical health will thank you sooner than later. Shhh! Enjoy the silence.

"Silence is a true friend who never betrays."

Confucius

SIT-IN

[sid in]

A public event where a person or group enters a place and refuses to leave until specific demands are agreed upon.

On February 1, 1960, the first sit-in took place in Greensboro, North Carolina. This demonstration by four courageous, young African-American men proved a pivotal moment in the civil rights movement. In the United States, the civil rights movement was a decade-long struggle to enforce constitutional and legal rights for African Americans that White Americans already enjoyed. Those four individuals' sit-in opened up opportunities for so many others to stand in places that would not have been possible had they decided not to sit-in. The movement was a decade long, and many lives of courageous people were lost for some who they probably never met. There was a belief in their heart, causing them to pursue legal rights they may never experience. A ten-year gruesome protest and sit-in – ten years and a countless number of lives lost – took place for them to be able to stand in places and be treated as human beings like White Americans.

I recall numerous opportunities I had to sit in areas of discomfort, intimidation, and disrespect from people who did not think I belonged in various conference rooms, offices, and positions of leadership because of my gender and skin color. Why did I sit in those places? It has never been my desire to sit-in or be out front, and titles were something I would shy away from. One day, one of my career mentors requested a meeting with me. She shared the story, and in our discussion, shared how she sat at many tables where she was not wanted and very seldom appreciated. When I asked her why, she said, "Everyone is not invited to sit at the table; for those of us who have the opportunity, we must sit in those seats for others coming behind us." I could have easily walked away. I stayed to honor the four courageous individuals who participated in that first sit-in so that I could sit down. I stayed for the generations coming after me; I stayed, and I sit so they can stand in the positions of change for generations to come. We sit so others can stand.

"Strong people stand up for themselves, but stronger people stand up for others."

Author Unknown

STEALTH MODE

[stelth mōd]

A cautious, discreet, and secretive way of moving or proceeding
intended to avoid detection, and a possible, customary, or
preferred way of doing something.

Stealth aircraft are designed to avoid detection using
various technologies that reduce reflection/emission
of radar, infrared, visible light, radio frequency
spectrum, and audio, collectively known as stealth
technology." Companies are operating in stealth mode to
keep whatever project or idea a secret for as long as possible,
before release. Some companies even give code names for
the project or idea so that it will remain a secret.

Have you ever shared a vision or dream with someone
only to regret sharing it due to their reaction? At that very
moment, you probably said to yourself, "I wish I had kept
that dream or vision in stealth mode." Not everyone is a
dream snatcher or vision buster. What am I saying? When
nurturing and building your dream or vision, remain in
stealth mode until it is time for revealing. Just as the stealth
aircraft is made with the capabilities to avoid visibility and
audibility, it is not seen or heard. So when you are in stealth
mode, speak details of your dreams only when necessary and
only listen to things that nurture your dreams and vision. Be

sure that your dream or vision is strengthened and solidified to repel the dream snatchers and vision busters. There will always be individuals who will attempt to snatch your dream or rip your vision apart, but never stop dreaming or envisioning. Maybe if your dream or vision is revealed, it will awaken something positive in those individuals for them to dream or envision again.

"Every great dream begins with a dreamer. Always remember, you have within you the strength, the patience, and the passion to reach for the stars to change the world."

Harriet Tubman

SUCCESSOR

[s k ses r]

A person or thing that succeeds another

In general business dialogue, I have often heard that everyone or everything should have a successor or a succession plan; if no plan or successor exists, you indeed will fail. I haven't fact-checked that against a person or organization; however, I agree that planning makes progress a smoother transition. It truly has for me. I can also attest to the fact that choosing a successor before needing one is beneficial, as it has benefited me greatly. I have never been threatened by sharing knowledge, something I call "paying it forward." During my thirty-five year career, I have, unfortunately, come across individuals who hoarded or withheld knowledge in fear that somehow sharing it would help others surpass them in their career. My philosophy is if I help someone get what they're seeking, generosity somehow will return to me.

Early in my career, I helped a young employee by sharing information that helped me and was shared with me by someone else. A more senior ranked employee asked, "Why are you helping that person?" You see, that young employee was several grades below me on the pay scale, something I found many measured a man or woman's worth by. I replied graciously, "I helped her because she needed help." The employee who made the disturbing comment of her being beneath me wasn't the only person made aware of the situation. Perhaps a month or so later, I was asked to sit in the executive office in the absence of the commander's executive officer. That is highly unlikely to occur when so many other individuals choose to, including the employee who had made the disturbing comment. The senior leader came out and said, "You're probably wondering why I requested you." I responded, "Yes sir," and he reminded me of the situation when I assisted the young lady who, by the way, had just joined his staff. She informed him of my help to her during her first week coming aboard.

You can only imagine the senior ranked employee's dismay when she walked into the executive office to meet with the senior leader and saw me sitting there. Quickly, she asked me why I was sitting there, and I responded politely. She attempted to downgrade my presence and said, "Have you made coffee?" Around that time, the commander walked out and said, "Kelly, I'm about to make coffee. Can I get you a cup?" She quickly ceased talking and found her seat in the waiting area until her scheduled meeting. I hope she learned the lesson I was taught in my youth and carry in my tool bag of success: a person's worth is never determined by what's on the outside of them but what they possess inside.

The lady I helped progressed up the rank rather quickly, and guess who ended up working for her and later replacing her. So that particular day I helped her, it was solely because she needed help. However, I also believe that on that specific day, a "life's succession plan," was set into place to become her successor, probably unaware to both her and me. I genuinely believe life has a way of paying forward goodness to continue paying forward to others. Look around you for your successor and look within you for your succession plan. Then coach and mentor someone who is not the next you but the next them at another level. Succession leads to success.

"Life is a succession of moments, to live each one is to succeed."

Corita Kent

SUSTAINABILITY

[s stān bil dē]

The ability to meet the present's needs, without compromising future generations' ability to meet their needs.

D o you have a personal sustainability plan? What exactly is that, you ask? A plan should include maintaining and improving our mental, physical, and financial health and actively supporting others to do so. Creating a sustainability plan for yourself can help create an impactful, positive lifestyle for yourself and others.

Money experts encourage us to set aside three to six months' worth of expenses in an emergency fund. This amount will sustain you in case an unforeseen life event arises. What amount of time or attention should we set aside, not merely to maintain but also to improve happiness' physical and mental sustainability?

Studies show that people, in general, believe success is equated to climbing to the top of a career ladder and making lots of money. A group of scientists studied approximately 100,000 lifestyles and found that making more money didn't bring them happiness, even if it got them the success they were seeking. According to the study, if having a successful career and money did not bring happiness, what did? More time. It is suggested that we work less and pay for services that will give us more free time. My current sustainability plan is relatively simple.

Presently, I daily carve out a little of my day for myself. Some days, it includes telling Alexa to play my favorite old school music and dancing like nobody is watching to end a challenging day. Another day, it could be having a slice of my favorite cheesecake and a glass of green tea after a hot bubble bath. It is during these sustainability times that I practice being fully there both physically and mentally.

I'm reminded of a precious lesson I gained from a flight. I paid attention to the flight attendant when she said, "The oxygen mask will drop from the overhead; put your mask on first before assisting others." I wondered why you would tell a parent not to assist putting on their child or elderly parents' mask first. Putting on your oxygen mask means taking care of yourself; they advise you to do so because if you run out of oxygen, you cannot help anyone else with their mask.

Each generation is responsible for taking care of their own without compromising generations' ability to take care of their own needs. We must ensure we do not handicap the generations to come by not sharing a sustainability plan that includes the history of how we overcame the perils of our past history. We must make them accountable by educating them about our history so they can develop their own sustainability plan and not fall prey to repeating it. We will put on our oxygen masks and then teach generations to come to put on their oxygen masks.

"Those who don't know history are doomed to repeat it."

Edmund Burke

TABLE

[tāb l]

A level surface on which objects may be placed and is used for purposes such as eating, writing, working, or playing games.

Individuals, like tables, are multifunctional. However, unfortunately, I think we fail to utilize all of our purposes. Why do you think that is? If I asked you to look at a table in your current environment, for what purposes are you using it? Allow me to go a step further. When you look into the mirror; honestly, can you say you are utilizing everything you have been purposed for? When it is leveled, my table is used for purposes such as eating, holding my books, journals, playing a few hands of spades, numerous rounds of dominoes, and sitting around the table with family and friends. It is utilized while sharing transparent dialogue that will hopefully help each of us on our life journey. Like the table, we often get cluttered by things placed on us, by others and perhaps ourselves. We then become weighted down, unleveled, or lose visibility of our authenticity. Yes, being multifunctional can be weighty and troublesome, especially when we no longer see our true identity.

Do not become weary in well-doing. Rest if you must, declutter, get leveled again, and clear things to the point you find your true self again. Do not make the mistake of quitting. Remember, at this point, if you leave any of your purposes on the table, it could leave a huge void in the lives of others. The part of the purpose left on the table could be the very thing the world is desperately in need of. For most of my adult life, I have wholeheartedly believed there is someone presently on the earth who has the cure for cancer. Maybe they got weighted down with a lack of funds to finish medical school or cluttered with choosing a career someone else thought was best for them and not following their purpose. Hear me and hear me well; if you are considering leaving any part of your purpose on the table, don't do it. The world is waiting for us to give out the things that have been deposited in each one of us. Muhammad Ali said, "Service to others is the rent you pay for your room here on Earth."

"If you decide that you're going to do only the things you know are going to work, you're going to leave a lot of opportunity on the table."

Jeff Benzos

TEACH

[tēCH]

Show or explain to someone how to do something.

I bet you still remember the name of your favorite teacher, the one whose teaching skills and nurturing techniques still resonate in your life today. I had many favorites, but my elementary literature teacher fits perfectly into this word. He was passionate about literature and teaching. His passion for literature spilled over into the classroom daily, and his teaching appeared to be two-fold. He taught us, and it seemed he was learning all over again with us. It was through this class that I fell in love with words, poetry, and essayists. On numerous occasions, I was drawn to Ralph Waldo Emerson, an American essayist, lecturer, philosopher, and poet. Emerson was quoted as saying, "He regretted that his teaching was perfunctory. He wished that he had shown his pupils the poems and works of his imagination, which he delighted in. The teaching might have been for himself also, a liberal and delightful art."

Perfunctory means of action or gesture, with a minimum of effort or reflection. Has anyone ever brought to your attention that you came across as perfunctory while teaching or instructing others? Do you believe you can effectively teach something that you have minimal to no interest in? I believe you can teach any subject to almost anyone; however, I ponder if the teaching will be effective, leading others to learn. I hold teachers in the highest esteem. I believe they're grossly underpaid for what they contribute to society. Before we were whatever occupation we currently perform, we were students first. I believe all humans possess life lessons that can be passed on to help others navigate through life. I challenge you never to stop learning, and after you learn, teach.

> **"Teachers affect eternity; no one can tell where their influence stops."**
>
> *Henry Brooks Adams*

TEACHER

[tēCH r]

Show or explain to someone how to do something.

A particular verse in the poem, "Our Grandmothers" by Maya Angelou caught my attention. It reads, "When you learn, teach, When you get, give." I overheard a conversation once where one asked the other, "Who is your greatest teacher?" The individual paused for a moment and responded, "My grandmother." Grandmothers are known to be precious jewels within a family, often called the matriarch of those families. A grandmother is an older, powerful woman within a family or organization who teaches words of wisdom to the generations coming behind her. Both my grandmothers, maternal and paternal, were my first teachers after my parents. Both of my grandmother's DNA is woven into the fibers of my being. However, it's the voice of my paternal grandmother, Naomi, that resonates in my memory slightly more for some reason. Grandmother Naomi was of Indian and African American descent. One of my unfulfilled dreams is to trace our family tree one day and gain more knowledge about her bloodline.

What I recall is she was a woman of prayer, a kind spirit,

and full of hospitality, sharing what little she may have had with others who were less fortunate. I started having this recurring dream about Grandmother Naomi and me a little over twenty-four years ago. The dream involved her walking through her house and carrying me in her arms, saying to me, "You are the generation that will see the answers to our prayers." I mentioned the dream to my mom, who was quite surprised that I would recall certain things about my grandmother since I was only a toddler when she passed away. I'm still unclear about the message or takeaway for the dreams. However, at certain periods in my life, I feel a push that I should be teaching when I learn something. Again, I am unclear about what that "something" is. I'm still seeking to find out what I have learned so I can teach what I have been given and give. I consider myself a student for life; it's fascinating to learn something new. In learning something new, I know a little more about myself and how I fit into humanity's equation. Never stop learning; the next thing could be the very thing that pushes humanity forward. Learn, then teach!

"Teachers affect eternity; no one can tell where their influence stops."

Henry Brooks Adams

TELOS

Greek: "end, 'purpose', or 'goal"

A term used by philosopher Aristotle, referring to the full
potential or inherent purpose or objective of a person or thing.

D o you believe that everything in existence has a
purpose? Aristotle, the ancient Greek father of
western philosophy, thought so. The first known
definition and use of the word telos was in 1904. I first
learned of the word on October 10, 2020, 116 years later, while
listening to a podcast about understanding your path to
success, owning your thoughts, and searching for purpose.
My fascination with words sent me on a journey to seek out the
meaning of something simple to solidify my understanding
of the word telos. I chose eyelashes. The eyelashes ladies'
role or purpose has been viewed as the emphasis of beauty;
however, their primary purpose is to protect our eyes from
small particles gaining entrance into the eyes and causing
harm. Why had I never thought to seek out the purpose of the
eyelashes before now? Probably the same reason so many
of us do not seek out our purposes in life until the moment
we do. I call those moments "aha moments," times when we
suddenly gain insight and realization of who we are and what
we have been purposed to do.

Why is it important to understand your purpose or goal in life? I believe a strong sense of purpose ignites your passion for achieving your goals. It is your internal alarm clock that goes off long before the external one does. Finding my telos and deciding to go after the achievement of my life goals has and continues to be a rewarding journey of personal growth. If you haven't started your telos journey, I challenge you to start it today. You will not be disappointed.

"There is one quality that one must possess to win, and that is definiteness of purpose, the knowledge of what one wants, and a burning desire to possess it."

Napoleon Hill

THANKSGIVING

[THaNGks iviNG

Public acknowledgment or celebration of divine goodness.

The United States celebrates the national holiday known as Thanksgiving, dating back 399 years ago in 1621. On this holiday, we first give thanks and sacrifice for the blessing of the harvest and the preceding year. Why do people annually celebrate Thanksgiving publicly on a particular day? Are we not a people, throughout the world, who give thanks every day? Who could have imagined, from the first observance traditions, that President Abraham Lincoln would proclaim it a one-time national holiday 242 years later on October 3, 1863. This came about after Sarah Josepha Hale, the woman who authored "Mary Had A Little Lamb," wrote letters for seventeen years to convince President Lincoln to make it a national holiday. Previously, in 1789, President Washington issued the National Thanksgiving Proclamation, setting in place "a public thanksgiving and prayer." However, it was also only a one-time event.

Sarah was an American writer, activist, and influential editor. A woman of significant influence and activism wanted a national Thanksgiving holiday, not just a one-time event. She believed the holiday would promote national spirit demonstrating prosperity and happiness for America. This would add a third patriotic holiday to the American calendar. Unfortunately, Sarah died on April 30, 1879, at the graceful age of ninety, sixty-two years before her dream was fulfilled. In 1941, Congress made Thanksgiving a permanent national holiday that would be celebrated on the fourth Thursday in November. Sarah believed this holiday would promote a national spirit of happiness and prosperity.

As I am writing this, it is November of 2020, and we are eight days from the celebration of the Thanksgiving holiday. As we near this holiday, we find our world still in the midst of a pandemic that we've been in for most of 2020. National and local medical professionals encourage us to keep our gatherings small or cancel gatherings altogether, as we continue to practice social distancing. We should certainly adhere to this wisdom of our medical professionals. However, we can still individually and collectively embrace the spirit of happiness, prosperity, and unity in our hearts. A very accomplished, influential activist who wore many titles wrote for seventeen years, and it yielded a national Thanksgiving holiday. What can we do in our families, communities, organizations, states, and world if we put pen to paper as Sarah did? What is something that will promote America and make a better world for all of humanity?

"As we express our gratitude, we must never forget that the highest appreciation is not to utter words, but to live by them."
President John F. Kennedy

THIRSTY

[TH rstē]

Having or showing a strong desire for something.

The Urban Dictionary defines thirsty as "too eager to get something (especially play)" or "desperate." It is said no one wants to be identified as thirsty; it is not a compliment. When you find women and men too desperate to gain your attention, be careful because their intentions may not be honorable. They may just be looking for a playmate – just plain thirsty. When we are so thirsty for a drink, we are not particular; we go for the first thing we can reach. Now once that thirst has been quenched, we have a choice for our next beverage selection. We don't take the first thing offered; we give some thought to our choice.

When we go after our dreams and visions, in most instances, our passion level is one-hundred. We have to be careful that we do not come across as thirsty. When a person appears to be thirsty, they will take the first drink that is offered. Growing up, my mom taught me that you don't eat from everyone's table; unfortunately, everyone doesn't have your best interest in mind. Therefore, I add that you also cannot drink from every cup offered. When you're on the path to your purpose, you cannot afford to drink from the cup of doubt, distraction, and derailment of your path. Make sure you stay hydrated with focus and self-assurance and remain steadfast on your purposeful path. Staying hydrated is crucial in keeping your energy level on point to pursue purpose. One of my mentors shared this with me early in my career, "Learn how to butter your own bread." Applying this to life meant not waiting for someone to do what I'm capable of doing for myself if I wanted something in my career. If a thirsty person approaches you, offer them the cup of "no thank you", and keep it moving.

"Appreciate water before you are thirsty! Appreciate all the good things before you need them!"

Mehmet Murat İldan

TRUTH

[tro oTH]

The quality or state of being true. A fact or belief that is accepted as true.

Reflecting on the word truth, "Stand in your truth" enters my mind, followed by the question, "What is my truth?" My truth starts with a foundation of faith and a structure, consisting of wisdom from past and present generations. Whenever success occurs in my life and people offer accolades, I thank them, of course. However, it's not my success alone; it is so much bigger than me. The words I share in this fifty-two week journey equate to a year but actually, many more than that; some I lived only through others' words—accolades to the generations who aided in establishing my truth. My grandparents birthed the words homegrown, baton, and successor and taught me to stay true to the innate gifts and talents naturally given by God. My parents birthed the words value, voice, and community. They taught me self-worth, to embrace my voice, and that I am never alone because I have community. With these valuable words deposited in my life, I stand in my truth.

"Find your truth and then live it."

Trudy Vesotsky

UNANSWERED

[n ans rd]

You have not answered or responded to.

T I am sure many of you have a list of unanswered questions like myself. Most of them start with "Why?" "Why me?" or "Why is this happening to me?" It does not matter if why stands alone or is followed by something that makes it more personal to your present situation. How often have you heard this question: why do bad things happen to good people? Or why did he or she do that particular thing? Many of the whys on my list may continue to go unanswered, and perhaps that is the way life would have it. I recall a line from a movie that said something like, "You cannot handle the truth." Maybe we wouldn't be able to handle the answers we are seeking if they were provided. Nevertheless, it does not stop us from desiring to have some of those unanswered questions on our minds answered.

In the last decade, there was a question that constantly remained on my mind. Why do we save things for a special occasion, as though every day in life is not a special occasion? I heard about a woman who was saving a dress for a special occasion. Many special occasions came and went, in her husband's eyes, yet she never wore the dress. Upon the woman passing away, the family was preparing for her celebration of life. Her husband looked inside the tiny storage chest and pulled out the beautiful dress. During the celebration of life, at her husband's first viewing, he smiled to see how beautiful she looked in the dress. He said, "Honey, this was my last chance at this special occasion you always talked about. I wish you could have seen how beautiful you look, and oh, how I wish we could have shared this first look together."

I drink water from my crystal glasses, and I eat my favorite grilled turkey and cheese with chips off my fine china. I even wear my favorite perfume to bed. Sometimes, the little girl in me still plays dress-up with no place to go, then I have a tea party for one. One may think the aforementioned is a waste or childish; I believe every day is a special occasion, and you cannot convince me otherwise. Suppose you're like the lady in my story, saving anything for a special occasion. In that case, I compel you to reconsider and look around, especially amid the pandemic, and start living every day like the special occasion it is. This way, you will not be like the husband in the story, left with unanswered why questions – questions like why she didn't see any of the past occasions as special enough.

"The most painful questions are left unanswered."

Susanna Dudiyeva

VALUE

[valyo o]

The regard that something is held to deserve; the importance,
worth, or usefulness of something.

What is the first thing that comes to your mind when you hear the word value? Most will say something monetary. I personally believe some items cannot be monetized, but many will disagree with my belief. Allow me to share a story regarding value.

Two people were walking in a parking lot. The first man saw an old penny lying on the ground, and he noticed it but kept walking. The second man saw the same old penny but instantly stopped, picked it up, and immediately became overly excited. The first man, only a few steps ahead of him, couldn't help but notice the man's excitement and turned to ask what was so exciting about an old penny. The man shared that he was a coin collector and that particular penny was worth thousands of dollars. He said that, in itself, was excellent news; however, what was more exciting was that it would complete his coin collection which was now worth millions.

You can only imagine the look on the face of the first man. He had judged the penny by its appearance and the value that had been assigned by the financial world. What is the lesson learned in my story? To the first man who had an unlearned perspective, the penny was just a penny. Now the second man who was an avid collector didn't see the penny as an old useless coin. He saw the possibility of a coin that had worth, could complete his collection, and could make the collection worth millions.

When was the last time you crossed the path of someone you considered less fortunate because of their appearance, and it crossed your mind that they might add something of value that was missing in your life? Probably never. Suppose this person had something of great value to add to your life, and you missed it because you did not see them as value added.

I remember when I was standing in a teller line eight years ago to make a withdrawal. A man behind me said, "Excuse me, ma'am, can I give you something?" I admit I was hesitant, but I agreed. He gave me a card that I still have today; the title is "And God Is Faithful." The card proved to be more valuable than any amount of money I could have withdrawn that day. I don't recall exactly what was happening in my life that I needed to be reminded of God's faithfulness; however, the card was so timely. He shared someone had given it to him at a vital time in his life and their only request was that he pass it on. He said the person told him he would know when it was the right time. He told me the same thing, "My only request is that you pass it on, and you will know when it is the right time." It has crossed my mind over the years, but I have not felt it was the right time. So until that time, I will continue to hold on to the card that brought much value to me that day. It continues to bring value each time I come across the card in my wallet, the place where I've kept it over the last eight years. To many, the card may be of no value, but to me, its value is far above any amount of money in my bank account. It was and continues to be a very timely and valuable lesson in my life. To me, the lesson on value will always be priceless.

"Don't educate your children to be rich. Educate them to be happy, so they the value of things not the price."

Victor Hugo

VICARIOUSLY

[v kerē slē; vī kerē slē]

Involves experiencing something through another person—you are not living your own life.

Our imagination is a powerful tool. When utilized correctly, it can build self-confidence, something that is necessary for all of us in order to navigate through life authentically. There is absolutely nothing wrong with admiring another individual's lifestyle or character. It is when we start to compare ourselves to others that the problem begins. Have you ever heard the statement, "Comparison is a thief"? When we compare our lives to others, it can distract us from creating and living our own lives. Have you ever found yourself imagining what it would be like to live a wealthy person's particular lifestyle? Perhaps you imagined what it would be like to drive that Bentley, live in a $750,000 house, and go on shopping sprees where price tags didn't matter.

One day, a friend shared how many people say they lived vicariously through him and expressed how lucky he was to be living the American dream. I went to what I thought was an overview brief; however, what he shared with me added to a valuable truth I learned as a young adult. Some of the most valuable things in life do not have a price tag. Now let me clarify that I'm not saying there is no cost, but that there is no price tag.

Okay, on to my friend's story, his goal was to become a millionaire in his mid-thirties. However, as he neared that goal, he went through a divorce and did not want his children to feel the pain from a decision they had nothing to do with. He voluntarily contributed additional funds, not court-ordered. The monies would've kept him on target to accomplish his goal of becoming a millionaire; however, he had no regrets in delaying his goal for his children. He went on to accomplish his goal fifteen years later, and he remarried, finally to the love of his life. They purchased their dream house, only to learn a couple of years later it was another facade. The marriage came crumbling down after learning it wasn't love but his money that she desired.

That day, I saw a very accomplished bilingual military officer, savvy real estate investor, and millionaire. However, I saw behind the smile and the brass on his shoulder, a man who had paid a cost far greater than the millionaire status he had acquired. His greatest desire was to be viewed and appreciated as an individual, not a price tag. Many ladies would call wealth "the icing on the cake." I use this analogy because if you grew up in the South, you know a cake doesn't need icing to be good. So if you find yourself vicariously living through someone else's life story, remember all the chapters may not have been released to the public. Go ahead and live your best, authentic life. You're the only one who can.

"Be yourself, everyone else is already taken."
Oscar Wilde

VOICE

[vois]

The sound is produced in a person's larynx and uttered through the mouth, as speech or song.

It is important to find and embrace your voice. In other words, own your voice; never allow anyone to minimize or misuse it. Your voice is of great importance. It can provide guidance in the time of uncertainty, dismiss assumptions that could bring harm, challenge prejudices, and so much more. I am sure you can see the damage that could be done if you fail to own your voice. Never be afraid or shy away from your voice.

In the world of technology, some devices grant access to a place or thing by voice; it is called voice activation. Can people have the same voice? People can share a similar pitch and certain vocal similarities; however, no two voices are alike when closely examined. Your voice, like your fingerprints, is uniquely yours. Have you ever been around a group of mothers with their children, and a child begins to cry or call out for their mother? You may see all the mothers pause and listen briefly. However, usually, only one mother will say, "Oh, that's my child." I've wondered how they know. Now I know there is similar pitch or certain vocal characteristics, but when closely examined, it is unique to that one particular child. Are you beginning to see how important your voice is now? There are certain sounds and words that I believe specific individuals have been assigned to speak. The same voice, depending upon how it is utilized, can encourage or discourage. Once words are dispatched, you cannot take them back. One of my elders often said, "Taste your own words first; listen to your voice. Is the tone acceptable to you?" If it is not, do not expect it to be acceptable to others.

While preparing for work travel, there was much discussion regarding if the trip should occur due to some last-minute labor and racial issues at the hotel where the meeting would occur. The trip was cleared; however, upon arrival, we were briefed that there could be some tension in the air. We were also told to maintain professionalism and decline any comments to the media if approached. Upon arrival, all seemed okay; on day two of my stay, one of the housekeeping personnel stopped me and asked could she say something to me. I paused but then said sure. She said, "We are excited you are here; we thought the team would pull out after hearing the unrest that was happening. We are glad you did not pull out, and thank you for being our voice at a table that we were not invited to." I smiled, thanked her for sharing, and then walked away with appreciation for having been allowed to communicate with an individual who did not think her voice mattered. So I repeat, never shy away from your voice; you never know whose life it will impact.

"We who have means and a voice must use them to help those who have neither."

Jennifer Donnelly

WALK

[wôk]

Move at a regular pace by lifting and setting down each foot in turn, never having both feet off the ground at once.

Joe South, known for his country soul genre, penned the song "Walk a Mile in My Shoes" that was performed by Elvis Presley in the 1970s. The lyrics went something like this, "Hey, before you abuse, criticize, and accuse, walk a mile in my shoes." How often have you heard someone say, "If I were you, I would do 'this or that'"? I have heard this so many times in my life, and initially, I remained silent. As I matured in life, I gradually started to respond.

I'm my own fashionista. I may purchase clothing designed by someone else, but I make them mine with how I wear them. Once, a person viewed a picture of me at an event and boldly said, "That outfit is so not you. Why did you wear that?" Here it goes... "If I had attended that type of event, I would have worn another outfit I know you have in your closet." I know you are probably in disbelief, like I was, that someone would say that to anyone. So how did I respond? How would you respond? I took her on a walk in my shoes.

First of all, the outfit was very nice, and the other outfit she mentioned was excellent also. I did not mention that

I had initially planned to wear that particular outfit she mentioned. I thought I would use this as a teaching moment, allowing her to "walk a mile in my shoes." I shared with her that I was notified by one of the event planners who learned of my attendance, that someone had shared my passion for mentoring. They wanted to know if it would be okay to sit me at the table with some young men who had a difficult start in life, recently found themselves on a better path, and was being recognized that particular night. I responded, "Yes, of course, I would be honored." These young men were all teenagers. The dress I initially selected was appropriate. However, I felt the one I changed to was more conducive to the atmosphere of my table audience that night. I purchased the dress because it was me, and I wore it for the same reason.

Be careful when people try to place you in a box they are comfortable with, instructing you to live out their perception of you rather than your authentic self. So the next time someone attempts to make the statement "If I was you..." or worse, you think of making the statement yourself, take a mental walk in their shoes before you abuse, criticize, or judge their decision. It is possible you do not have enough information to entirely understand their decision.

"Walking a mile in someone else's shoes isn't as much about the walk or the shoes; it's to be able to think like they think, feel what they feel, and understand why they are who and where they are. Every step is about empathy."

Toni Sorenson

WHITE SPACE

[(h)wīt spās]

The areas of a page without print or pictures

I first heard the term white space in a military environment from my previous Army Commanders. Sitting in a meeting during a morning synchronization session, both military and civilian leaders were going around the table synching their calendars for the upcoming week. I kept hearing, "He doesn't have a lot of white space this week." I was puzzled, but I dare not ask the definition when it appeared that so many others apparently understood the term and frequently utilized it. After the meeting, I learned through research that the definition was "free time or availability on his calendar."

White space is not often heard outside of a military environment. Why not? It is certainly a term we can use in governing our personal lives. For example, when the phone rings on your self-care day, you can politely say, "I regret I don't have any more white space today." Now be ready to explain if the person on the other end doesn't comprehend.

While attending an innovative writing class, the instructor's ice breaker was, "What do you see?" while holding up a blank sheet of paper. The instructor's response was your legal space in the class to do whatever you chose and take ownership of it. Kind of like the Commander's calendar, although many were speaking how much white space was or wasn't available, the ultimate decision was made by the Commander. He could have disagreed with what others thought was enough white space for him that particular week, and in many instances, he did disagree. Why did he make changes? The short answer is because it was his; he owned it.

Too many of us, in our personal lives, allow other people and things to fill up our white space based on their measurement of what is enough. Ultimately, the final decision is up to us. We own the right to say how much white space is enough for our day, week, month, or even year. Guarding your white space is crucial. Set healthy, wholesome boundaries for yourself and others, and take ownership of that white space. I often hear people say "protecting my peace," but today, I remind all of us to protect that white space.

> **"Singapore gives 10% 'white space' time to all of its teachers to come up with their own innovations outside of the official curriculum."**
>
> *Andy Hargreaves*

WHY

[(h)wi]

Say something to obtain an answer or some information.

The day I found my "why" was the day I found myself, unrestricted and free to be totally me. It was important to identify who I was to myself first, then to others. Perhaps you ask why to yourself first. If I did not identify with who I am to myself first, I would run the risk of serving others a counterfeit me rather than the original me.

How does one identify with them first? I started with a conversation with myself. I asked my younger self, my foundation, my core, and my value system, what is your expectation of me? I was provided with one response: to never forget her. Who was the "her" being referred to? The happy little girl filled with innocence, always seeking the good in others, and never allowing anything to minimize her self-worth. I have kept that promise to her to this very day. She is etched in the fibers of many adult life decisions. To others and myself, I serve the authenticity of the little girl in me, still looking for the good in others, and the woman who recognizes the bad. I am making life decisions to stay true to us.

"To thine own self be true!"

William Shakespeare

ACKNOWLEDGMENTS

A quote that is woven into the fabric of my being is the African Proverb "It takes a village to raise a child," I am that child, and I am grateful for my village of Family, the Harvest & Toney, Alabama Community, Inner Circle, and Mentorship of the National Organization of Blacks In Government (BIG). I am an indeed a reflection of my village; when you see me, you see them. My goal daily is to reflect my village in excellence.

A special thanks to my village for continuously challenging me to become the best version of myself.

MEET THE AUTHOR

Ms. Charlesetta Kelly Brinson is a native of Harvest, Alabama. She is grateful for the opportunities her life has afforded her, beginning with becoming the mother of two lovely daughters and grandmother of five grandchildren who she affectionately call "The Little People." Followed by over 30 years of dedicated service to the Department of Defense (DoD), a career where she served her Country alongside the Air Force, Army, Marine Corps, Navy, and Corps of Engineers as a DoD Civilian. She is a licensed Minister of the Gospel, a product of Sparkman and Lee High School, J. F. Drake Technical College, Albany State University, Defense Acquisition University, Darlene H. Young-USDA Graduate School, Leadership Academy School, and is presently studying at Liberty University. She is the Founder and CEO of Gen3 Life Coach & Consulting LLC. She is a servant at heart and passionate about equipping others to become the best version of themselves, walk in purpose, and leave the world better than they found it.

STAY CONNECTED

Thank you for reading, *Path to Purpose.* Charlesetta looks forward to connecting with you. Here are a few ways you can connect with the author and stay updated on new releases, speaking engagements, products, and more.

FACEBOOK	@gen3CoachKelly
INSTAGRAM	@gen3CoachKelly
TWITTER	@gen3CoachKelly
EMAIL	gen3CoachKelly@gmail.com

Made in the USA
Columbia, SC
29 April 2021